Life in Colonial America

PETER F. COPELAND

DOVER PUBLICATIONS, INC.
Mineola, New York

DEDICATION
For Andrew Mathieson

Bibliographical Note

Life in Colonial America is a new work, first published by Dover Publications, Inc., in 2002.

DOVER *Pictorial Archive* SERIES

This book belongs to the Dover Pictorial Archive Series. You may use the designs and illustrations for graphics and crafts applications, free and without special permission, provided that you include no more than four in the same publication or project. (For permission for additional use, please write to Permissions Department, Dover Publications, Inc., 31 East 2nd Street, Mineola, N.Y. 11501.)

However, republication or reproduction of any illustration by any other graphic service, whether it be in a book or in any other design resource, is strictly prohibited.

International Standard Book Number: 0-486-41861-8

Manufactured in the United States of America
Dover Publications, Inc., 31 East 2nd Street, Mineola, N.Y. 11501

INTRODUCTION

In 1492, Christopher Columbus sailed with a commission from the government of Spain to discover trade routes to the Far East and India (hence, the naming of the Native American inhabitants of the New World as Indians). This was the critical moment in the exploration of the Americas, as word of Columbus's voyages spread and other Europeans joined in the search for trade routes. Eventually, expeditions set out from Europe for the purpose of colonizing the "New World," with Spain, Portugal, England, France, and the Netherlands taking an interest in the vast continent. From furs and fish to cedar logs and sassafras, the varied opportunities for trade and profit prompted many expeditions.

The appeal of the new land was not limited to economic reasons, however; then, as now, people were drawn to the new land to escape religious persecution or to worship as they pleased (the Quakers in Pennsylvania, Puritans in New England, Catholics in Delaware, among others). Of course, many settlers hoped to better themselves economically, and many did, working the land or joining the booming tobacco trade in the Chesapeake region.

Life was difficult, however, for the common people who lived in colonial times, many of whom arrived on these shores as bondsmen, indentured servants, transported criminals, and slaves. Relations with Native Americans were often hostile. The death rate among colonists was high, as they succumbed to illnesses such as malaria and dysentery. Food was often scarce, and medical care was lacking or negligent.

This book depicts many aspects of life in colonial America before 1776: how the colonists lived, dressed, and traveled, along with some of the events leading up to the forging of the new nation. Beginning with the passage to and arrival in the New World, the book concludes with the signing of the Declaration of Independence. Various colonists and adventurers are depicted—the Dutch, the English, the Swedes, the French in Quebec and the northwest, and the Spaniards in the areas that are now Florida and California. The Native American inhabitants, and the African slaves who were brought over to serve the landowners and work the land, are depicted as well.

A passage to the New World, early 1600s. The thirteen colonies that would eventually become the United States lay along the Atlantic coast of North America. In the early seventeenth century, the English began arriving in wooden sailing ships such as the *Mayflower*, seen here. The ships were crowded to capacity with seekers of new lives in a new land. The arduous journey from Europe to North America took several months.

Arrival in the New World, early 1600s. The Virginia colony at Jamestown, founded in 1607, was the first successful English settlement in America. Other colonies were founded in Massachusetts, Connecticut, Rhode Island, Delaware, Maryland, Georgia, the Carolinas, and Florida. Here we see the *Mayflower* passengers arriving on the rockbound shores of New England.

Encountering the Native Americans, early 1600s. Upon arrival on the shores of North America, the Europeans were met by Native Americans. Many of the early colonists were not adept at farming, hunting, or fishing, and if not for the friendly Indians who taught them the techniques of survival in the new land, they would have starved to death before the crops they had been taught to plant had grown to maturity. Here, a group of disembarking colonists catches sight of the Native American inhabitants.

Spanish settlement at St. Augustine, Florida, early 1600s. St. Augustine was the first settlement established by the Spanish north of Mexico (1565). It was for many years not much more than a military camp— it was one of a chain of forts built to protect Spanish shipping in the Caribbean Sea—but it has survived as the oldest city in North America. Here we see a street scene in the plaza of colonial St. Augustine.

The lost colony. English explorers, searching for a sea route to China, landed on the coast of Virginia in 1587, where they established a small colony. Three years later a returning English expedition found the colony deserted, the only trace of the vanished colonists being the letters CRO carved in a tree trunk, and the name CROATOAN carved upon a palisade near the gateway to the deserted colony. Among those missing was Virginia Dare, the first child born to English parents in the colonies.

Building houses at Massachusetts Bay Colony, 1627. Nearly all of the colonists' homes in the New England colonies were built of rough logs hewn into regularly shaped timber; the houses had thatched roofs like those in small English villages of the time. Walls were constructed of woven branches plastered over with mud. The colonists shown here are busily thatching a roof.

6

Clearing land and building houses in the Maryland colony. In February 1634 the Maryland colony was established along the Potomac River near the estuary with Chesapeake Bay, where the city of St. Mary's was built. The first houses were simple wooden cabins, but brick houses soon replaced them.

7

New Sweden, 1638. A colony of Swedes was established along the banks of the Delaware River in 1638. The colonists built Fort Christina near the present-day city of Wilmington, setting up log cabin dwellings of the type customarily built in their native country. These simple houses, which could be constructed using no other tools than axes, eventually became the prototypes for the American frontier log cabin.

A Dutch patroon and his wife, ca. 1640. The patroons were Dutch citizens who agreed to bring settlers to New Netherland in exchange for land. Many owned great estates in what is now upstate New York. Here, the patroon wears breeches and doublet of rich velvet. His soft felt hat is decorated with ostrich plumes. His wife wears a silk gown of red with cuffs and ruff of starched lace, as well as an apron of fine Holland linen.

Puritans of the Massachusetts Bay Colony, 1640. The dress worn by the Puritans of Massachusetts Bay was sober and restrained, both in color and cut. The religious Elders controlled such matters, and everybody dressed according to what the Elders ordained to be right and decent. In the second half of the seventeenth century the ordinances of the Elders carried less weight, and the fashions popular in London came into favor. Children's clothes were fashioned upon the same patterns as those of their parents.

A colonial bedroom. In the simple one-room houses built by the early colonists, the family slept in a bed built into one corner of the room. Children's beds were kept under the parents' bed, to be pulled out at night; the baby's cradle was set at a safe distance from the fire, although close enough to take advantage of its warmth.

11

A colonial kitchen. The kitchen was the warmest and most comfortable room in the colonial house on a cold winter day. The atmosphere might be enlivened by a rich venison stew bubbling in an iron pot in the large brick fireplace, along with a pair of rabbits browning slowly in the iron broiler below the hanging kettle. A musket and a powder horn might be hung within easy reach above the fireplace.

12

A colonial shipyard, 1650s. Ships were in demand, especially for voyages home to England and to the West Indies, and every colonial seaport had one or more shipyards. American merchants shipped their cargoes aboard American-built ships, and English shipowners were happy to be able to buy American-built ships for about one-third the cost of those built in Europe. American-built ships would in years to come dominate the oceans of the world.

Dutch New Amsterdam, 1653. The Dutch established a fur-trading station at Albany on the Hudson River in 1614, but it was not until 1623 that the first trading post was established upon the island of Manhattan by the Dutch West India Company. Depicted here is the thriving seaport of New Amsterdam, capital of the Dutch colony of New Netherland, as it appeared in 1653.

A post windmill. The windmill, introduced by the Dutch at New Amsterdam, had two types in colonial America. The more common "post" windmill, shown here, headed its sails into the wind while rotating upon a huge center post, balanced by a beam-mounted wheel that revolved as the mill turned. The second type, the "smock" windmill, differed from the post in that only the mushroom-shaped "cap," or top, of the mill revolved with the changing winds.

Sir William Berkeley, royal governor of Virginia, and Lady Berkeley, 1675. Sir William Berkeley's harsh rule was addressed in a 1676 document drafted by the people of Virginia—growing class distinctions, high taxes, and a perceived bias toward the Native Americans had alienated Berkeley's subjects. Nathaniel Bacon led an anti-government movement, Bacon's Rebellion, in June of 1676, demanding reform from Berkeley and the House of Burgesses. Several months later, Bacon and his men burned down Jamestown. The Royal Governor is shown here dressed in red, with gold-laced buttonholes, buttons, and binding on his black hat. Lady Berkeley wears a pale blue dress trimmed in white with white apron and sleeves.

An ox team, ca. 1680. The ox was the original beast of burden in colonial America. Ox teams were used for all sorts of tasks, such as gathering hay in summer meadows; spring plowing; hauling rocks and tree stumps from cleared fields; and taking sap from sugar maples in the northern colonies in springtime. Ox teams could still be seen on New England farms until well into the twentieth century.

A hunting party, ca. 1685. Early colonial farmers supplemented their often meager diet by hunting the abundant wild game in the fields and forests. This provender often was all that stood between the early settlers and starvation. For later colonists, hunting became a sport. Here, a group of gentlemen hunters are out for an afternoon of sport with their dogs.

An early Pennsylvania farm home, 1680s. This mountain cabin, built of rough logs with the bark left on, could be quickly erected with a minimum of tools, as could the split rail fence. A stick-and-mud chimney was built outside and above the fireplace, which had been constructed of rocks. The rifle-wielding farmer, clad in a rough homespun hunting shirt, is on his way to hunt game for the table, assisted by his dogs. The farmer's wife can be seen boiling hog grease and lye in water to make soap for the family.

Indian slaves in Charles Town, South Carolina. By 1685 the port of Charles Town in South Carolina was busily exporting deer skins to England, as well as Stono Indian slaves, taken in the interior, whom they sent to the slave markets of the West Indies. Soon, however, rice would become the great crop of the South Carolina low country, and African slaves would be imported from West Africa aboard slave ships to replace the Native Americans, who had sickened in the malaria-infested rice fields and died.

On the deck of a slave ship. The importation of Africans from the slave coast of west Africa had become a large-scale business by the end of the seventeenth century; it continued in ever greater numbers until the slave trade was outlawed in the early nineteenth century. Slaves were bought and sold in all of the thirteen colonies until the time of the American Revolution, when the trade was largely forbidden in the northern colonies. African slaves, such as those shown here, were regularly brought up from below decks and made to exercise. Crew members used whips to urge on the slaves.

The Deerfield Massacre of 1704. The town of Deerfield, Massachusetts, was twice raided by French soldiers and their Native American allies, once in 1675 and again in 1704, during the colonial wars carried on by France and England. Those inhabitants of the village who were not slain on the spot were marched north to French territory in Canada. The village minister, the Reverend John Williams, was allowed to return to Massachusetts, where he wrote an account of the events. Here, Abenaki Indians attack and burn houses in the town during that winter night in 1704.

Colonial dressmaking. The working dress of the poor was simple and well made, often constructed of coarse fabrics and homespun materials. The dress of the well-to-do, however, might be made of velvets, brocades, and silks, edged with gold and silver lace. Here we see a lady being fitted for a gown by two seamstresses. The clothing was almost always made to order—there were very few garments to be purchased ready made, and these were mainly for poor laborers such as sailors or slaves. This lady's dress is of striped silk, with fine Holland linen sleeves.

Slaves in a southern plantation kitchen. The plantation kitchen was a building separate from, but built near to, the plantation house. The wall contained a fireplace with a swinging iron crane, upon which pots and kettles could be hung directly over the fire. Corn was the mainstay of the diet; it provided food for the family and servants and was also brewed into homemade beer. Meat was preserved by salting and smoking it in a small house behind the kitchen (the smokehouse). Well-to-do people of that time were hearty eaters, and colonial planters were no exception. Here we see house slaves at work preparing the evening meal.

24

A horse race. Horse racing had become a popular sport in the American colonies in the early years of the eighteenth century. The *Boston News-Letter,* in its August 29, 1715, edition, contained the news of a horse race for a purse of one hundred pounds. Other popular colonial sports were bowling (bowls) and football, which was played in Massachusetts as early as 1686.

French *voyageurs* in the northwest forest, 1730s. The French had begun exploring the North American interior as early as 1604, and soon were taking home from Canada furs worth thousands of crowns. Samuel de Champlain founded his first settlement on the St. Lawrence River in 1604 and began a brisk trade in beaver pelts, which were highly valued in Europe. Soon the *voyageurs* (travelers) of New France were pushing westward in pursuit of the lucrative fur—trapping, trading, and concluding alliances with the Native American tribes, while exploring the Great Lakes and Hudson Bay and the Mississippi and Missouri rivers.

A sailors' tavern in Boston, 1735. In colonial days, the tavern not only furnished food and lodging for travelers and horses, but also provided refreshment and amusement to neighbors. It was a meeting place where news could be gathered. Taverns were the centers of life, where even a royal governor might be seen, and carousing and roistering were not strenuously forbidden. Shown here is a sailors' tavern in Boston, where a young man might be directed into a life of adventure aboard a Man of War [naval warship] or a Privateer [armed pirate ship] during one of the colonial wars of the 1700s.

27

Bringing tobacco to market. Tobacco had been the money crop of colonial Virginia and Maryland since the early days of those colonies. Tobacco was moved by water to European markets; the ships that transported the crop were docked at the wharves of large plantations located along river fronts. Smaller planters moved their crops to the wharf along a "rolling road"—a trail created by slaves continually rolling huge casks of tobacco leaf by hand, horse, and ox to the plantation wharf, where the tobacco was loaded aboard Europe-bound ships.

Reading the newspaper, 1740. Newspapers began to be printed in Europe in the late seventeenth century, and soon after that in America. The colonial reader could get the "latest" news (weeks old, in fact) from England, as well as news from other colonies and accounts of laws passed in Parliament relating to colonial life and trade. The few newspapers that existed in the colonies were eagerly passed from hand to hand, especially in smaller American towns and villages. America's first newspaper, the weekly *Boston News-Letter*, was launched in 1704. In the years leading up to independence, the demand for news increased, and the number of newspapers did as well.

George Washington as a young surveyor. As a boy, George Washington was instructed in the art of surveying. He carried out much of his work along the western frontiers of Virginia. Lord Fairfax, a wealthy landowner, commissioned Washington to survey the boundaries of his estate; Washington was later appointed surveyor for Culpepper County, Virginia. The young George Washington is shown here surveying with Benjamin Banneker, the African American who became an eminent mathematician, astronomer, and inventor. Trained as a city planner, Banneker was instrumental in designing Washington, D.C.

Urban crime in Philadelphia, 1755. Crimes committed by the desperate and destitute were less common in the American colonies than in Europe. In the new world, a poor man—if he were free and white—could live above the crushing poverty that afflicted the lower classes, especially those entrenched in the cities of Europe. However, urban crime did exist. Depicted here is an incident that reportedly took place in Lombard Street in Philadelphia in 1755—the assault and robbery of a gentleman by two chimney sweeps.

The funeral of General Braddock, 1755. During the French and Indian War, the colonists supplied colonial regiments that fought alongside the English against the French and their Native American allies for control of North America. General Edward Braddock, commander in chief of British forces in North America, was killed in battle at an ambush set by the French and their allies. Although highly skilled in European military tactics, Braddock lacked knowledge of the wilderness. George Washington, the colonel of the Virginia regiment, attended the funeral of Braddock (shown here) and led the battle's survivors back to the safety of the English settlements.

A Dutch wagon, 1750s. Most travel by land in the colonies was limited by very poor roads and few bridges; transport by water was preferred wherever possible. Early land transport was carried out by pack horses and wagons such as this "Dutch" wagon, a forerunner of the great Conestoga wagon, drawn by six or eight horses, that appeared after the American Revolution. The Dutch wagon was used to haul farm produce, supplies, and farm equipment, among other cargo. The wagon was smaller and less rugged than the Conestoga wagon.

Quebec, 1759. The British and French fought five colonial wars between the years 1689 and 1760 to determine who would control the future of North America. The British conquest of Quebec in 1759, and the French surrender of Canada to the British by the Treaty of Paris (1763), ended these conflicts; Britain and Spain became the major colonial powers on the continent, with the Russians in control of Alaskan territory. Pictured here are British officers and a lady in the streets of conquered Quebec, which shows the evidence of damage from fire and British shelling.

A frontier fort, 1760s. The first structure raised by the early colonists in the new land was a fort. Forts were built to protect the colonists from European rivals who might seek to take over the colony, as well as from incursions by hostile Native Americans reacting to the colonists' intrusions into their hunting lands. Many forts eventually became trading posts and meeting places for travelers. Shown here is a stockaded fort on the Virginia frontier in the 1760s.

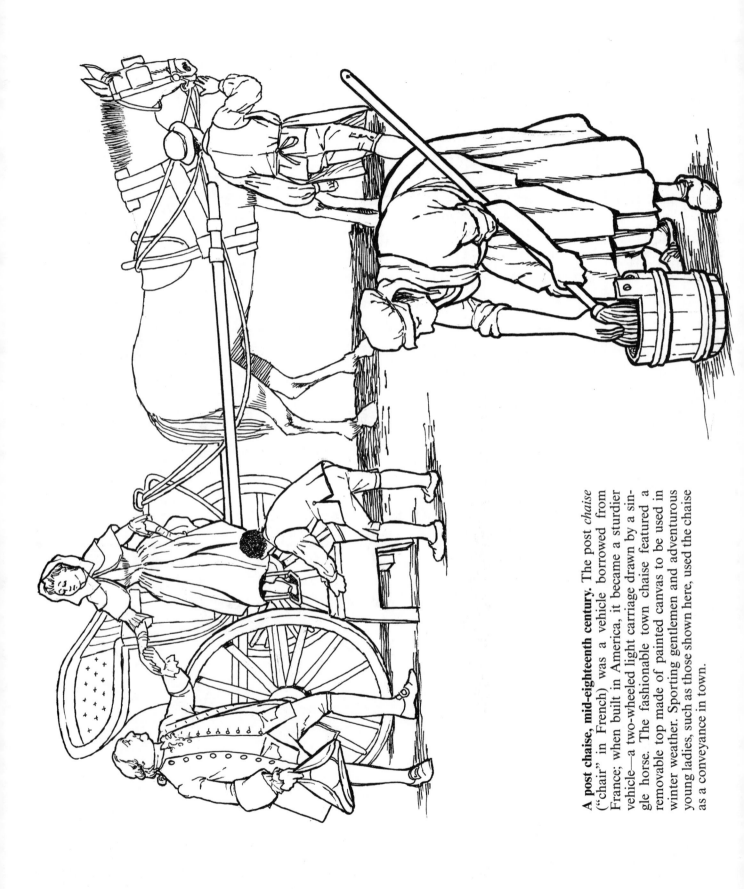

A post chaise, mid-eighteenth century. The post *chaise* ("chair" in French) was a vehicle borrowed from France; when built in America, it became a sturdier vehicle—a two-wheeled light carriage drawn by a single horse. The fashionable town chaise featured a removable top made of painted canvas to be used in winter weather. Sporting gentlemen and adventurous young ladies, such as those shown here, used the chaise as a conveyance in town.

A Native American fort in the Appalachian wilderness, 1765. In some remote mountain areas, where settlers were few, a Native American fort might be erected on a hilltop, perhaps overlooking a few valley farms. The fort was essentially a two-story log cabin with gaps between the logs so that riflemen could fire through them. A Native American fort might be a residence or only occasionally tenanted when warfare was expected. A few such buildings still stand in western North Carolina and southwest Virginia.

A river ferry, ca. 1770. As roads were improved, bridges began to be built across narrow streams. The bridges usually were nothing more than logs laid across a stream from bank to bank with boards or limbs laid across them. Rivers were crossed by flatboat ferry. Usually a local landowner added to his income by building and operating a ferry, a shallow rectangular scow [flat-bottomed boat] built wide enough to accommodate a horse and wagon, and, perhaps, a small number of cattle, horses, or oxen.

A stage wagon, ca. 1770. The stage wagon was the ancestor of the stagecoach. It was a vehicle with a wagon bed and box, equipped with backless benches for passengers. Only the few early arrivals got to sit in the rear of the wagon, where they could lean back against the frame of the wagon box. Generally, nine passengers were carried inside, and a tenth sat in front with the driver. Leather curtains could be rolled up on each side, or let down in bad weather; there was no heat or window glass to protect the passengers in winter. The stage wagon was an altogether uncomfortable conveyance, and the later stagecoach was not a great deal better.

A Spanish priest in California, 1771. Although Spain had laid claim to California since the sixteenth century, it had done nothing with the territory except to allow the Catholic church to begin missions to the Native American inhabitants. It wasn't until the 1760s, with news of Russian expeditions down the western coast of North America, that the Spanish begin to establish armed settlements between Los Angeles and San Diego. Shown here is a priest at Mission San Antonio, accompanied by his Basset hound, among the local children.

Lamplighter, ca. 1775. Only the largest colonial cities had street lights; installation began in the years preceding the American Revolution. Philadelphia, for example, had street lights installed and operating by 1762. In addition to lighting lamps in the evening and extinguishing them at dawn, the lamplighter also was responsible for cleaning the lamps, trimming the wicks, and filling the pans with oil each day. Shown here is a lamplighter filling the oil pan of a street light in Philadelphia.

Militia muster, 1775. Each colony possessed a militia in colonial times. The militiamen drilled and practiced upon the village green under the direction of an officer, usually a prominent citizen who claimed some military experience. This practice continued long after the colonies became states and would become an American institution. Here, patriotic citizens practice the evolutions of musketry drill upon the eve of the American Revolution.

Pulling down a statue of King George III, 1776.
Differences between Britain and the colonies had
become increasingly divisive after the last of the wars
with France had ended, and, by 1775, fighting between
British troops and American patriotic forces were
increasing. Resentment and hostility toward the
"Mother" country and all things British led to the
destruction of symbols of British royal authority. A
New York City mob is shown pulling down a statue of
King George III in 1776.

The signing of the Declaration of Independence, 1776.
Finally, after a year of open warfare, the leaders of the
patriotic forces in the Continental Congress approved
the Declaration of Independence on July 4, 1776. This
historic document announced to the world that the
thirteen former British colonies in North America
were henceforth independent of Great Britain and
self-governing, thus bringing to an end the colonial
American experience and the birth of the new United
States. The signers shown here are, at left, Benjamin
Franklin; seated, left, Thomas Jefferson, and right,
John Adams; standing, John Dickinson.